Things Boundaries are Allowed to Do for Youth Groups

(An Incomplete List)

Ben Kucenski

Things Boundaries are Allowed to Do for Youth Groups

(An Incomplete List)

Paperback Edition: 979-8-9939525-3-6

Copyright © 2025 Ben Kucenski

All rights reserved.

No part of this publication may be reproduced, stored, or transmitted in any form or by any means without the prior written permission of the author, except in the case of brief quotations used in reviews or scholarly work.

This document is not about suspicion.

It is about responsibility.

Section 1: Things Boundaries Are Allowed to Interrupt

Focus: Harm depends on uninterrupted access.
Interruptions prevent harm before it begins.

Boundaries exist to stop situations early —
before anyone is confused, pressured, or isolated.

Boundaries are allowed to interrupt private conversations

Boundaries are allowed to interrupt "just checking in" messages

Boundaries are allowed to interrupt prolonged one-on-one time

Boundaries are allowed to interrupt emotional dependence

Boundaries are allowed to interrupt secrecy

Boundaries are allowed to interrupt exceptions

Boundaries are allowed to interrupt favoritism

Boundaries are allowed to interrupt spiritual authority used for control

Section 2: Things Adults Are Allowed to Notice

Focus: Harm is revealed through patterns, not moments.

This section names what adults may notice over time — without guessing motives or reading minds.

Adults are allowed to notice who always volunteers for isolation

Adults are allowed to notice who resists accountability

Adults are allowed to notice who dismisses policies as "legalism"

Adults are allowed to notice who needs to be special

Adults are allowed to notice grooming disguised as mentorship

Adults are allowed to notice emotional intimacy crossing roles

Adults are allowed to notice when rules only bend for one person

Section 3: Things Policies Are Allowed to Be

Focus: Harm thrives in flexibility.
Clear policies reduce opportunity.

This section frames safeguards as care —
not distrust, suspicion, or fear.

Policies are allowed to be inconvenient

Policies are allowed to override charisma

Policies are allowed to override seniority

Policies are allowed to override spiritual gifting

Policies are allowed to protect adults as well as children

Policies are allowed to remove discretion

Policies are allowed to make misconduct harder, not impossible

Section 4: Things Grooming Is Allowed to Look Like

(So It Is Not Missed)

Focus: Grooming rarely looks alarming. It usually looks reasonable.

This section names familiar, ordinary behaviors — so harm is recognized early, not excused later.

Grooming is allowed to look kind

Grooming is allowed to look spiritual

Grooming is allowed to look like rescue

Grooming is allowed to look like favoritism

Grooming is allowed to look like trust-building

Grooming is allowed to look boring

Grooming is allowed to take years

Grooming is allowed to involve parents

Section 5: Things Adults Are Allowed to Say Out Loud

Focus: Clear language interrupts manipulation.

This section gives adults permission to speak plainly — so silence does not carry the burden of safety.

Adults are allowed to say "That makes me uncomfortable"

Adults are allowed to say "That's not appropriate here"

Adults are allowed to say "We don't do that alone"

Adults are allowed to say "That crosses a boundary"

Adults are allowed to say "Policy matters more than intent"

Adults are allowed to say "This needs another adult present"

Section 6: Things Harm Commonly Relies On

Focus: This is about systems and conditions — not villains or monsters.

This section names common patterns quietly and clearly, without exaggeration or fear.

Harm relies on trust without verification

Harm relies on reputation

Harm relies on being needed

Harm relies on adults wanting harmony

Harm relies on fear of accusation

Harm relies on adults assuming "someone else is watching"

Harm relies on confusion about consent and maturity

Section 7: Things Children Are Never Responsible For

Focus: Responsibility belongs entirely to adults.

This section makes that clear —
so harm is never explained away, minimized, or misplaced.

Children are not responsible for adult boundaries

Children are not responsible for adult self-control

Children are not responsible for clarity

Children are not responsible for resisting authority

Children are not responsible for reporting perfectly

Children are not responsible for understanding grooming

Section 8: Things Churches Often Get Wrong

Focus: Confusion creates space for harm.

This section names common misunderstandings — clearly, calmly, and without accusation.

Confusing forgiveness with access

Confusing repentance with restoration

Confusing calling with entitlement

Confusing growth with intimacy

Confusing trust in God with lack of oversight

Confusing silence with peace

Section 9: Things Safeguarding Is Allowed to Cost

Focus: Prevention has a cost.
So does harm.

This section prepares leaders to choose safety even when the cost is real and uncomfortable.

Safeguarding is allowed to cost convenience

Safeguarding is allowed to cost volunteers

Safeguarding is allowed to cost money

Safeguarding is allowed to cost reputation

Safeguarding is allowed to cost comfort

Safeguarding is allowed to cost growth

Section 10: Things Adults Must Agree On Before Working With Youth

This section names shared commitments —
clear, practical, and non-negotiable.

These agreements protect young people,
and they protect the adults who serve them.

We do not create secrecy

We do not rely on private communication

We do not override policies for compassion

We do not confuse spiritual authority with personal access

We intervene early

We support adults who raise concerns

We remove access before we investigate intent

www.ingramcontent.com/pod-product-compliance
Lightning Source LLC
Chambersburg PA
CBHW060532030426
42337CB00021B/4225